THIS IS WHAT THEY SAY

DEAD END

M. BARTLEY SEIGEL

THIS IS WHAT THEY SAY

M. BARTLEY SEIGEL

Distribution by Typecast Publishing.

Library of Congress Control Number: 2012944733

ISBN 978-0-9844961-4-3
SECOND EDITION

Edited by Jen Woods
Designed by Typecast Publishing
Cover photograph by M. Bartley Seigel

Printed in the USA

For the people and places in Montcalm County, Michigan,
from a time when I called it home.

Strange country, this ragged, roiling rage.

Good children don't swim in dead lakes. They don't congregate like cigarette butts along the line of sand and water. Good children don't stare too long into the darkness or ask questions they shouldn't. They don't play on pavement cracked and weed-choked or shade themselves in the shadows of creaking vats or idle along chain link long enough to draw attention to themselves. Good children don't drink from cloudy water or wade for minnows and frogs in the shallows—there are no minnows and frogs in the shallows. Neither are there summer dances upon the island like long ago when the young strung lights from the branches of trees and small boats ferried girls in white toward music and laughter across the water. Nothing is across the water. Good children know this and do as they are told.

There are places to hunt, places to hide, and love clicks on and off like a lighter. Love is another word for we-the-people. Sometimes we're all flowers. Other times, we're an exultation of larks. Kissing each other's bodies, we cross our wires to test our hearts and heartbeats. All huddle and quake, we lie with fingers inside one another, whispering aphorisms into each others' cauliflower ears. When we sleep it is half-sleep and when we dream it is half-dream burned on its side. In the mornings, we arise from our musk like children. In rolling waves of laughter, we rise to greet our days.

We lie sullen in the dark, arms thrown over our eyes, breathing in the other's breath. It takes no small process to dislodge ourselves from each other, our sheets, to cross the floor barefoot without upsetting floorboards or children. Then kettles, faucets, stove tops, cups, refrigerators, cartons of bad milk, all our little explosions. This is a kind of seduction, too, though we seldom see it. We are all paper dolls. We are all scroll work and the creative use of light. Out the window there's fog on the hills while inside there's the smell of chicken bones, cat boxes, kerosene, the coffee burning. In our pubic beards, the smell of each the other's body. But all we can think is avoidance and even this thought-crab crawls out our ears, out through our half open windows while we stand there, dead in our skins, hands limp at our waists, watching our dreams disappear into the darkening trees.

Just about everyone, just about everything begins with a lump, in the belly, in the armpit, in the throat; nodes on a branch that become leaves that die and drift to the ground leaving bare limbs under a dusting of snow. Play something dirge and drudge, trot out the pipes, the strings. Make a show of forefinger and thumb—*ain't that how it goes, the world's smallest, tiny-like?* Mostly, it's just a second ago and she's across the table, sipping a beer, smoking a cigarette, pushing a greasy hair behind her greasy ear. Then she isn't. Mostly things are like this. Not holy, just hollow.

Love is made from laughter, tears, fists, and forgetting. Blood gone scab is the richest portion of a garden picked to the bone. Iron, wine, and behind that nothing, no one, ghosts. The sun sets and in the distance dogs begin to bark. A child is lost. Something is forgotten and left behind, like distance, like time, like avoidance, like denial. A grave is dug. Head trauma, gut shot, or running a snowmobile through barbed wire, or turning a tractor over in a ditch, or falling headlong into a swollen river, or just a tumor, nothing more. How long will each of us lie pondering the sky while our waters run out, while leaves pile up, while love is made?

Our mornings won't always be like this. We'll do our little time, save our little money, and find some place where we can't be found, where we can lie in bed until noon staring at the cracks up in the ceiling. There, our skins won't tear or burn or bruise and our ears won't ring. There, we'll learn to listen to mice in the cupboards, to birds in the bare branches outside our windows, to our hearts and our heartbeats. We'll learn to build a fire and bask in its brittle flame.

We swelter in a brittle kettle under a black setting sun. They say the doors have fallen from the hinges and our clocks have stopped. Our mothers no longer speak. Flies gather. We bend spoons with minds lock-jawed and rickets-bound, crucifer in staccato, our pale tongues clicking and whirring, breathing thirst into our fairytales, sparking brushfires, and ghosting these once wooded trails, these once bountiful orchards with dreams painted in thunder and antimony. Our bodies will be pulled from these lakes, glistening, woundless, and beautiful, like we want everything for ourselves, like we are everything.

In our basements we become aware that the scars on our knees aren't those from third grade when we fell from the merry-go-round, something only our mothers will remember, but something darker, some emerging other self, hiding just beneath the surface. We see it in each other's eyes. We imagine we hear voices from upstairs, voices from blocks away, not some super human ability, but part of a new us waiting to erupt forth. And the sweaters lumped in the corners aren't our sweaters, but something alien and protean, some earlier shell shed. And our bodies bent one over the other aren't our bodies, but those of some other entity entirely, introducing us to the interior of our dark futures. We won't own up to this, but we'll rent it for a while until the dreams subside.

Mouths to feed, mouths to wash out with soap, mouths to fill with words that can be thrown back at us like bricks. The garden has gone to weeds, the garage needs painting, the brakes on this truck will give any second, and it has all been so long coming, so much anticipated, that it will end as an enormous exhalation of relief. We must learn to be hungry, to keep company with our hunger, to learn what it means to drive directionless in pursuit of something gnawing, empty.

Sometimes we open our mouths and our fathers and mothers crawl up from out of our throats. They grasp at our teeth and lips and pull themselves up like babies from a birth canal, peaking their heads out, roaring like hungry little bears, their gasoline voices wrapped in barbed wire, lit matches in their tight little fists. Sometimes we can heal ourselves, perform the necessary triage, but most times we can't. We misread the nature of our wounds and woundings, applying leaches to black eyes, trying to kiss away slit wrists. We imagine ourselves the kind of people who don't lie or steal or break hearts or bones.

All sallow-faced and boney-skulled, we laugh at our hairy potbellies and share another cigarette, hopeful that if we put away our pocketknives long enough we'll end up in bed, shouldering each other's weight around our soiled sheets. We'll false promise to walk the line and pretend we've no intention to hang ourselves. That's some kind of sad song, isn't it, come to rest on its hands and knees, head hung low? Let us sing it out, lucky in our love like old radios on windowsills, our dusty vacuum tubes still warming at the pinch of electricity, our volumes turned up too loud, too strong.

We keep trying to locate ourselves in these woods, between the trees, behind woodpiles. We descend into our swamps, duck into our dark closets, pull our hair shirts over our heads, hide behind our calloused hands. Outside gas stations we smoke the butts of discarded cigarettes, one after the other, looking over our shoulders for women informants and men from our pasts. Shadows, darlings, our mothers and fathers, sisters and brothers, children and dogs, ex-lovers and current, preachers and parole officers, their ghosts threaten to discover and overcome us.

If we haven't yet drawn up our last plans on yellow legal pads, we should. If we haven't yet sawed off the barrels of shotguns and filed down the bores, we should. If we haven't yet packed away cartons of canned goods under our beds, under our stairs, up between the rafters above our foundation walls, we should. If we haven't yet said our prayers, counted our blessings, taken stock; if we haven't yet made this list and burned the evidence and reassembled the evidence from the ashes and weighed out the shoddy merchandise, now might be a good time to start.

When we hurt, songbirds nest on our shoulders and vines send tendrils up our legs lest we float upward to whatever heaven awaits us, our souls departing to the clouds and sky forever.

Over the horizon is another horizon. Down the dirt road is more dirt road. Some dreams deserve to be run down, others to die. We should all learn to tell the time.

Love is homespun stitches and the Thorazine shuffle, all buckets of nails, rickets and spider, rabid bit, and strapped to a gurney. Laugh it off, love.

Shivering in the morning light, we gather like cigarette butts at the water's edge, our thousand naked bodies in a long chain bent from burden and burnt to the filter. What we've learned. Scars are replaced with more scars. Hair grows up from scorched earth. Once, we would have cut ourselves with broken glass, that the wind might rush through the breach to line us with fallen limbs and leaves. But beach sand has since worn dull the sharper edges of our pain. Stomachs empty and growling, we've come at last to these shores copper-wired, gear and pulley. All coiled spring and iron will, our words tintyped on our tongues, we clasp arms and dive into this thing together, electric and beautiful as bullets. We disappear beneath the lake's surface for what seems a grateful eternity, knowing somewhere out beyond the tree line's dark reflection, where the water is cool and clean and clear, the long arc of a sandbar awaits.

No longer delighted by the velocity of crows, by the dirt under our own nails, by our preacher's fragmented ravings, we've become bored as cattle and can't sleep. The braying of the congregation sends us walking down the line to stand in the mildew of the irrigation spray that our sins might wash away. Carrot flower and hard candy, oil shale and whiskey bottle, we speak only in tongues, wide open to fear, to joy, to trouble, come whomever, whatever. Standing in the first rays of the morning sun, drunk on turpentine water, we'll grab anger by its buzzard wings and wave a solemn goodbye.

Ours are tallow plants, stamp mills, rail yards, feed lots, hardscrabble farms at the edges of things, nowhere sliced thin to the bone. Mnemonic geographies, these outer rim reminders where in clapboard houses dirty-faced kids get high on an alchemy of state statistics. Incarceration, suicide, pederasty, homicide hides behind it, just out of sight, out of mind, and chicken is for dinner. Penny candy arcade fire at the Five Corner Store, bang, bang, and we wander aimless down these derelict stretches of dirt road where the muddy margins team with castings. The school bus driver is a preacher thrown from the pulpit for what only children leering out the emergency door window, hoping to catch an eye, can tell. Give those kids a wave. Much depends on it.

Between a factory for plastic bits and one for brass bones is a parking lot cracked and weed-choked, and behind that another and another, on down to a dirt patch of bins, dumpsters, barrels, piles of machine excrement, and then the brown ribbon of an oily river flanked in willow and scrub oak. Black crows, silent moons, orbit above the traffic of our children's bodies, watch their comings and goings, insistences and acquiescence, their quarrels, apologies, and excuse makings. The birds see what we deny, but hold their brittle tongues, content in knowing what we cannot, and refusing to share the news.

We lick our fingers and feel for air, hold up mirrors searching for breath, and build better birdcages in which to kill our canaries. In this place we are all dead, pawing blind like a zombie through a junk drawer, searching among leaching batteries and rusted thumbtacks for a lost key. Sticks and stones may break our bones, but the second part is a dodge. It's the words that creep up through the floorboards at night in a cold draft. Words are the clattering of bare branches in the trees, the clicking of a blind man's cane. Tapping out the code, little dirty words like little dirty birds failing to fly south for the winter, sticking close to pick at our eyes. It brings us down like a bolt gun at the end of a long, narrow chute. On the killing floor, we will be fleshed and hung to drain out our ink, our words rattling to the bottom of an abandoned mine.

Our survival knives are all we'll need to make it in this wilderness. We'll be at the saplings with them all day, carving sticks for tiger pits, cat ears nestled like raisins in the hollow handles beneath our broken compasses. A whirling, white-eyed, shirtless violence scratching its balls and sniffing its fingers, we'll call you fag or ragged fucking cunt, then take our stitches silently in the kitchen with sewing needle and fishing line, a cigarette lighter, a little whiskey to wash the weeping wound.

Cracked porcelain dolls, cutters and bleeders, bored as cattle, we sit in the weeds at the edge of our fallow fields. Under a sky like a cold trencher, smoke and ash, our third eyes watch for black satellites orbiting like crows. We are collapsing stars, all gamma and radio pulse, not birdsong. Our voice burlesque, our wild-eyed whispers are like shards of glass, like barbed wire buried in the meat of trees. Terror embroidered; lock-jawed and dissembling, we are nightfall, thunderhead, mushroom cloud. Like a shockwave rippling across a darkening plain, our gravity is a dance, beautiful as a bullet. We bring down disaster no less now than ever, always and never simultaneous, like a river beyond its banks, undeniable and insidious.

Effective immediately, applicable in all our states, we are subject to search and seizure. Should we wish to report our loss, our damage, or delay, we may do so loudly, publicly even, but we won't be heard. Should we persist, our hands and faces will be present for cuffing. Our shortness of breath, our blurred vision, our predilection for sweets and violence, our gradual slipping into trancelike catatonia, these are markers of our ineligibility. Restrictions, inscrutable charges, perpetrated by a system beyond our command—call it God—will be applied.

They die and we want to put our anger in a pill we can pull open at will, snort or cook for a needle. We want to take over, but we're too busy smashing and peppering, too busy burning and punching out teeth—*what the fuck are you looking at?* As small children, we'd bite the edge of the kitchen counter and hang there by our heads, arms limp, legs dangling. The marks are still there. We'd hide in our bedrooms, under every blanket in the trailer, imagining the smells and colors of today.

We mark our maps in musk, dust, wood smoke and urine, disoriented to the polar star. We stumble into our open topographies in pain, in rage that won't kindle, won't burn, our oxidation too slow for the tasks at hand. We move through these landscapes as if we weren't born to them, as if these hills and valleys weren't our very own, as if we were lost and cannot be found.

Wrap the next hour in rice paper and care. Too few for a bestiary, we sacrifice our birds before they make nests. Little gatherings, little instruction sets, we rummage around. Sometimes life is pit fruit. Sometimes we chip our teeth. Just keep the naming at eye level, keep our eyes on the prize, keep everything tight like woven jute. Poised upon this rocky ledge, persisting like cats at a feather under a door, we guard our cabinets of curiosities like our lives depend on it because our lives depend on it. We cradle this single blue egg in our palms, all soft procedure and secret will. We nestle in for the kindling sound.

We shed our clothes like leaves from a tree, less mirror than doorway, a visage less ourselves than goose flesh migrating across vast expanses of skin. Our flock reveals more than human terms allow. Splashed against the backdrop of stunted shrub and lichen, our chimera's mouth, stifled by feathers, cannot be heard by closing the eyes. Instead, the eyes must squeeze shut, tighter and tighter until the creation of their own white light and the blood roaring into our ears conjures fire, different from conjecturing fire. This is synaesthesia, our correction, necessary like pinching ourselves, hard between thumb and forefinger over and over, is necessary for us to summon up from the hot thrum of our bodies the shushing sound of waves and threshing wind. This place we call elsewhere, anywhere but here, a northern lake, where we swim out beyond the tree line's reflection to a place we know cannot be depended upon. Here we will release our buoys from their chains that we might display our illuminated objects.

In the shadow of the sawmill, of the chemical plant, of the grain silo, of the potato barn, in the mud, in the mind, shout, bellow, borrow, steal, testify. Get a belt, get a switch, knock heads, black an eye, puke blood. The gnashing of false teeth—*save me Lord*. On a three-wheeler, buried under Old Style, a man can in one hand, a child in the other, a pig fucker, a dirt farmer, a dirt ass, slipshod, snot-nosed, pinch-lipped, and pucker-mouthing, Bible banging, face punching, and crank smoking, truck stop whores rolling hoses from pickup tailpipes into a John's bedroom window, putting a pistol to an ear, a shotgun in the mouth. Neither running, neither feared, never mind, you, son. We're pounding ham-handed on the glass—*for the love of Christ, get that balloon out of your mouth like I told you or ain't nobody going to the Dairy Queen.*

They say not to speak of negatives, like the roof falling in, or the bottom dropping out, but we wonder what then to speak of. Sermons, half jokes, inscrutable instruction, what frightens us most are the rotting beams invisible beneath the floorboards, the threatening collapse from above. We consider the possibility of unperceived existence, we consider the dissimilarity between sensation and reality, but there is little to do but sigh deeply and return to our exhausting toil, knowing in the deepest recesses of our collective heart that night terrors are for children and we are all too awake.

It hurts, this walking, weeping wound, this cleaning up with whiskey, this burning what's left in a fifty gallon can. The draw between is slow and tight. Keep it close, shut, together. Keep it in the family, like our mouths and minds. Together, we'll bleed this pig of its bad blood.

There are traces of laughter in the sky, but mostly silence. Locked safe in our basic cells, our hearts refuse to release their holdings. Like little echo chambers, all disconsolate recombination and recrimination, our halos are etched in stone and bone, hunched and knock-kneed. We threaten to jump, to stub out our little burning embers, to trail off and disappear like tendrils of smoke, but in the end we do no such thing. Instead we persist and survive because we must. The dead don't hear apologies and the living need more than words.

We've got good figures for people our age, kids at home, a little good money on a good night twenty-five freeway miles to nowhere. It's a hard thing to pass on, these parts. Trucker's pockets packed with cash in chain-strung wallets. Our bare limbs pay the bills, keep the lights on, keep milk in the fridge, sure things. And when the music starts we'll just close our eyes, close them tight like we've kept our mouths. We'll imagine a northern lake, tree-lined and ancient, maybe a city we've never seen, a dark hive. We'll imagine places where we can breathe or hide or both and some way, we will get there.

We don't dress in gingham and tulle, not linen, but in shadow, alum, and ghosts. We dress like action figures, our figures ready for action, all super bendy knee and kung fu grip, our detachable backpacks filled with secrets no one can decipher. All broken glass and turpentine, our souls fold in on themselves like paper cranes, satyr butterflies, like lightning on the horizon.

Our lidded heat is handed down, handed across the table, across the polished oak, traded like horses and cards. We know this, know blood into bruises and the numinous eye. We know the body's daily failings. We spoon peas onto our plates, onto Mama's best china, while our little unknowable minds tie knots and paint the horizons of our souls in golden sun.

Camel filters and the back of a stranger's hand, we'll close our eyes and pretend we are peach, blackberry, brandy. We'll pretend we are sparrows. Something about this morning with its bombed-out buildings and empty windows. Something about this day with its silent, gray faces and still, huddled shoulders. In our bones we feel the air leaving us. In our bones we feel our fish blood cooling, congealing. Pretend we are hard candy, butterscotch and peppermint. Pretend we are a first kiss and the end of days.

Bus wheels roar over freeway concrete under a sickle moon. From our seat in the back, from deep within our jailed bodies, in our belly's hollow breath, we feel for that vast hidden space tucked somewhere within our molten core. We dwell near our pendulous hearts where heaven's blue waters lap at the edges.

In bed, eyes closed, all diabetes and high blood pressure, we feel at the white wires growing from our ears. Smart on our lips the abdomen kiss. Who needs mouth talk, all tongue and spit, our lungs full of sulfur smog and nicotine, our heads full of fantasy? We want to retire these dry eyes, these thoughts like fat hen's eggs and get back to something resembling sleep.

Withdraw, push away, cross our hands on our chests, say our prayers. We'll quit smoking and keep each other from killing. We'll quit coffee and keep each other from killing. We'll quit drinking, Jesus, quit books and start our sunburned lives over. Under our pillows we'll keep the ache in our teeth and the longing for each other's skin, our ten thousand noticings of shore and forest, none of which can contain us like we might contain one another. After dark we'll swim naked in black water. Then, wrapped in blankets, we'll sit on the porch and watch the snow descend into our hair.

How to hang a door, hold a chainsaw, hammer a nail. How to butcher a hog, chance a guess, hazard a chance. How to build a barn or bed a woman. How to make her come. How to clean a carburetor, change a light bulb or a tire, tie a knot or a tie. How to birth a calf. How to dig a grave. How to bury a baby. How to plant a garden, build a fence or a fire. How to unclog a toilet, ease a broken heart or staunch the flow of blood. How to pluck a chicken, pay a bill, aim a shotgun. How to boil water, dry tears, salt the earth. How to win a war, shovel a path, point a well. How to split a log, square a post, read a book, kick a dog. How to weather a storm. How to write a song, which is to say, how to follow a trail.

Like a symphony gone wrong, we dance naked for each other, a promise of future promises. The music frightens and we imagine our bellies as white sacks of spider eggs. Watching each other watch, we doubt our own cheap movie, the husk of things.

We leap from our chairs like men shot to pull at the nearest hair. If the phone rings, we don't answer it. We discipline ourselves through the hatred and anger, convince ourselves that it will all finally pass. We are giddy with this misconception and our determination will demand its own destruction. Meanwhile, we endure.

We are young and tall and thin and beautiful and all of our friends will be jealous. We'll drive to Tennessee to see about a job, and late at night we'll stop to drink coffee and eat donuts at a gas station along the highway. There will be bands of stars and dark curves through low hills and country songs on the radio. We'll drive long after we've admitted to having to pee and this will become a joke between us.

No one has money. No one has food. We have our skins and our hunger together instead. The trees sway in the wind. The neighbor's dogs bark and bay. We creep down to the river, wade into its water and fill our buckets with crayfish and clams to put into our bank accounts, by which we mean our bellies. We can't afford new clothes. We can't afford electricity. We can't afford to care so we pick leeks and dig cattail roots and hunt for mushrooms. We fix the trailer with corrugated tin we stole from a collapsed barn. We adopt every stray dog that crosses our paths because we're fools.

The snow won't subside and the pipes have frozen. There's water in the basement and the rats swim. The wood is green and the chimney fire is all that's keeping us warm. Everything the end of the world should be and more. Snapped tendons. Bleeding gums. Cows in trees. Sheet metal peeled off roofs like bananas, like oranges, like apple rinds piled high for pie. We scream, but nobody can hear our voices. In winter it's snow and wind. In summer it's rain and wind. Come fall, leaves. Come spring, gluttons for our punishment, some of us are back for more.

This year of abundance, this cornucopia of desire, corn in the cribs and hay in the lofts, babies milk-fat in their baskets. There's work in the mills and fields and there's money to be had and spent. The women put on make up and the men all loosen their collars. There are picnics and parades and the school gets a fresh coat of paint. The grass is tall and game is thick in the woods. The rivers are full, but not high. The fish run on time. The wells don't run dry. This, too, happens.

No one can ever truly know what will happen. Storms kick up dust and demons. New moons cast their brittle light on our excesses, our excuses. Windows board up and children fly south like birds at the onset of winter. We are all cutters and bleeders. We are all of us destined to end where we began. We are all of us saying this all of the time though none of us seem to hear.

We clasp arms and dive in together. When we emerge we are mahogany, slippery meat and heat, uncomfortable in our flesh in the chill morning air. The invitation of fresh conscience and muscled thought. By August we'll have forgotten one another. By August our bed sheets will have been burned and we'll have mere seconds to hide.

Ours is this sky inside the orb of heaven, no other. Cupped within our palms, our fallow fields sleep-swaddled in blankets of snow and ice while under the earth sleep our dead. Life knows us and hovers about our knees. Trapped in a fear relentless as wild dogs, we can still attempt a crossing. We may sense our own end, but we can still move through these wooded hills, our minds attentive to the contours of the land.

Drunk to be teased from our dark shells, pushed over our darker edges, killed even, we end up liking each other more than we supposed we might. Nobody else is there to guide us through this, no one cares. Stinking, our incogitant attitude, our pockets empty, our backs broken, we're left alone to stumble arm in arm from shining castle to shining castle toward the last best place on earth, simple, pure and terrible like little gods.

Disconcerted and heartbroken, our waters run in perfect time and measure. We find it pretty, even as it chills our feet. Well used, our lives will resemble trenchers piled with bones well-picked, grease congealed in the cold-edged light of dawn. Confusion and resentment might linger near the bottom of our cooled kettles, but something beautiful happened here once, something boiled and steamed, and the scent of our tallow, our sweat and musk, will hang on in the air for a while after we've gone.

The moment comes, but all in silence, turning in the tide and drowned in other rushings. Our convictions earnest, our passions unhinged, things fall apart easily and quickly. But once, when the worst worked its seduction and we succumbed, turned in its maw, on its tongue, our sinews torn, our bones crushed, we found our centers weren't lacking. Everything was panic and waking Benzedrine nightmares of lost work and penniless boredom, of scattered, wayward children. We slouch toward our cheap salvations in whatever way we can, trigger fingers crossed, sight hairs against the blowing gale.

Our ghosts are not benevolent, protecting us from minor disasters. Untamed, unnamed, we understand them to be the spirits of cancers, bad hearts, and they walk whispering to our walls. They stand next to our washing machines in our basements, sit on the counters of our kitchens, watch us measure out coffee and bleach, dress our children, squeeze toothpaste, climb into our sheets. We know they are watching, that they care for us like no one else ever could.

Skinny and little, we know things. We know to avoid the boys on the playground and their menacing sports. We knows they'll pursue us into the scrub trees behind the school. We know no one will come to our aid. We know the stones in our fists offer no more real protection than words save their small satisfactions. The words we'll keep to ourselves, just as the boys will keep their own as they toe the voodoo line we draw in the dirt with our crazy eyes.

Doesn't matter how big you are if you've got the crazy eyes, our uncles whisper. They'll think twice. But the boys will just pause there under cover of the trees, the musty dank of early September clinging to their skins. They'll pause just for the toss, stand their distance just long enough to best weather our little hail, fists clenched, faces pinched in malice, and then they'll come on, just as we know they must.

We'll learn to laugh with our mouths closed. We'll learn to lie in wait. Watching and patience are weapons. This is what they say.

After the terrible argument we will make love and afterward lie sullen on the bed, our bellies down, heads turned away. Life is all beyond us, and we will get up without speaking, without so much as a sigh, and go into the bathroom to draw a warm bath. We will listen to the sound of the splashing water.

ACKNOWLEDGEMENTS

Someone once wrote that to write poetry is not a personal achievement. I wish to acknowledge my family and friends for their infinite patience and love, especially my wife, Marika, and my kids, Annika and Indrek; thank you. A heartfelt thanks to Typecast for believing in the words. especially to Woodsy for her gift of sight. Thank you to all the poets and writers and musicians whose voices have been my constant companions and from whom I've undoubtedly learned all of it. And last, but not least, some of these poems or parts therein had previous life in the pages of *The Lumberyard; Alligator Juniper*; *Bateau*; *Bluestem*; *Cellpoems*; *DIAGRAM*; *Forklift, Ohio*; *H_NGM_N*; *Michigan Quarterly Review*; *Monkey Bicycle*; and *Wheelhouse*. Thanks to the editors for giving me an audience.

M. Bartley Seigel is the founding editor of the critically acclaimed literary magazine [PANK].

He lives, writes, and teaches in Houghton, Michigan, where he is assistant professor of creative writing and diverse literatures at Michigan Technological University.

www.ingramcontent.com/pod-product-compliance
Lightning Source LLC
Chambersburg PA
CBHW031139090426
42738CB00008B/1157